PUPUS . . . again

adaptations by Sachi Fukuda

Bess Press
P. O. Box 22388
Honolulu, HI 96823

Cover art by Jason Teraoka
Sachi Fukuda
Pupus: Again
Honolulu, Hawaii: The Bess Press, Inc.
128 pages

Printed in the United States of America
ISBN: 1-880188-56-2

Dedication

To my dear husband Lynn
who has made my retirement
such a joy!!

PUPUS. . .again *is my second effort at publishing recipes collected since 1983 when* **PUPUS: ISLAND ADAPTATIONS** *was first printed.*

This is a compilation of recipes tested and adapted over a period of 30 years. A few are original recipes which were developed through trial and error.

And for those who worry about not being able to cook, if you can read and follow instructions, you can cook. I did not cook until I got married and did so only because we had to eat. So, don't give up, hang in there and try different recipes. Where there's life, there's hope. Good Luck!!

TABLE OF CONTENTS

Dips & Spreads

ANCHOVY VEGETABLE DIP

2 cans flat anchovy filets, well drained
¼ cup red wine vinegar
¾ cup olive oil
4 cloves garlic, minced or pressed
¼ tsp. pepper
½ cup parsley, chopped

Place anchovies and vinegar in blender and whirl until pureed. Add oil, garlic and pepper; whirl until smoothly blended; stir in parsley.

Transfer to a serving bowl; cover and chill at least 2 hours. Yields 2 cups.

NOTE: Good with celery and cucumber sticks, radishes, cherry tomatoes, whole mush-ooms, broccoli and cauliflower. Chill vegetables also until serving time.

This is an exotic dip which you will love once you try it.

The original recipe called for 3 cans of anchovy which was too salty for my taste so I cut it down to 2 cans.

GLORIOUS MUSHROOM SPREAD

2 Tbsps. butter
1 lb. fresh mushrooms, diced
1 large onion, chopped
1½ cups mayonnaise
10 strips bacon, crisped, crumbled
½ tsp. seasoned salt
½ cup Cheddar cheese, grated, optional

In large skillet, sauté mushrooms in butter 3-5 minutes. Combine with remaining ingredients and bake in flat oven-proof dish at 350° for 20-25 minutes. Spread on cocktail rye rounds or crackers. May be assembled up to 2 days ahead and heated before serving.

NOTE: Freezes well. Thaw, warm and serve.

ARTIFICIAL CRAB DIP

½ lb. artificial crab
½ cup small curd cottage cheese
1 cup mayonnaise
½ tsp. seasoning salt
1 2-oz. pkg. Ranch Style dressing mix
½ tsp. garlic salt

Cut artificial crab strips into 1 inch pieces, shred. Mix with remaining ingredients, chill and serve with crackers or vegetable sticks.

AVOCADO-CRAB DIP

1 large avocado, diced
1 Tbsp. fresh lemon juice
2 Tbsps. grated onion
1 Tbsp. Worcestershire sauce
4 oz. cream cheese, softened
½ cup sour cream
½ tsp. salt
1 7½-oz. can crabmeat, drained and flaked

Mix diced avocado with lemon juice, onion and Worcestershire sauce. Stir in cream cheese, sour cream and salt. Add crabmeat and mix thoroughly.

Serve with tortilla chips or crackers.

NOTE: Use firm avocado to avoid a messy looking dip and toss rather than mix with lemon juice, etc. Blend the cream cheese, sour cream and salt, add the crabmeat and fold carefully into the seasoned avocado.

You will enjoy this once you get past its looks. Good change of pace from the usual Guacamole Dip which everyone prepares whenever avocados are plentiful.

Here again you find grated onion being used in a dip.

CHEESE JELLY SPREAD

8 oz. cream cheese, softened
1 10-oz. jar pineapple preserve
1 10-oz. jar apple jelly
3-4 Tbsps. horseradish
White pepper to taste

Blend above ingredients except cream cheese and pour over softened block of cream cheese. Serve with wheat crackers.

NOTE: There should be enough horseradish so you can taste it. This is a refreshing, delicious dish and can even be used as a dessert.

It also makes a large quantity, so you may want to half the recipe if serving a small group.

COLD SHRIMP DIP

1 8-oz. cream cheese
1 cup small shrimps, cooked
¼ cup mayonnaise
½ cup chili sauce
¼ cup grated onion
3 drops Tabasco
½ tsp. Worcestershire sauce

Beat cream cheese until smooth, fold in remaining ingredients and mix until well blended. Refrigerate for several hours. Serve with Ritz Crackers or raw vegetables.

NOTE: Freezes well. Handy for unexpected company.

HOT CLAM SPREAD

2 7½-oz. cans minced clams
with juice
1 cup bread crumbs
½ cup butter, melted
½ tsp. oregano
½ tsp. parsley flakes
Dash of garlic salt
Dash of salt and pepper
4 oz. Mozzarella cheese, grated
½ cup Parmesan cheese

Combine all ingredients, except cheeses. Place in 9" oven-proof dish, sprinkle with cheeses, bake at 350° for 15 minutes. Serve with crackers.

8-LAYER DIP

1 can Jalapeno Bean Dip
1 large avocado, mashed with
  1 tsp. lemon juice and
  Green Taco sauce to taste
3 Tbsps. mayonnaise
3 Tbsps. sour cream
1 Tbsp. chili powder
1 cup Jack cheese, grated
1 cup Cheddar cheese, grated
2-3 cups chopped firm tomatoes
4 stalks green onion, chopped
1 small can chopped olives

Spread Jalapeno Bean Dip on large flat serving dish. Cover with seasoned mashed avocado.

Cover this with mixture of mayonnaise, sour cream and chili powder. Add Jack and Cheddar cheeses.

Cover with chopped tomatoes and green onions. Top with chopped olives. Use taco or corn chips for dipping.

NOTE: Have a spoon handy to scoop this delicious dip on the taco or corn chips. Dip is quite stiff and heavy so the spoon will help.

There are many variations of this dip but I like this best of all. The men seem to like this heavy, filling dip.

HOT BROCCOLI DIP

4 scallions, diced
2 Tbsps. butter
1 pkg. frozen broccoli, chopped
1 can cream of mushroom soup
¼ lb. fresh mushrooms, chopped
8 oz. Cheddar cheese, grated
¼ tsp. garlic salt
3 dashes Tabasco
¼ tsp. pepper
½ cup toasted slivered almonds
1 loaf thin Pepperidge Farm bread

Thaw and drain broccoli.

Trim crusts from bread and cut into squares or triangles. Bake in 250° oven for 1 hour.

Sauté scallions in butter. Mix in remaining ingredients and cook on low heat, stirring frequently until it boils.

Transfer to chafing dish and serve hot. Use toasted bread squares for dipping.

NOTE: This can also be used as a dip for raw vegetables.

LOMI SALMON DIP

½ lb. salted salmon
1 small round onion
2 medium, firm tomatoes
Poi

Rinse salmon a few times and soak at least 2 hours. Drain and remove skin and bones. Cut salmon into ¼-½-inch strips and then into cubes.

Cut round onion and tomatoes into similar-sized cubes.

Use 6-inch skewers and skewer a piece of onion, tomato and then a piece of salmon.

Place in spoke-fashion on a flat platter with a small bowl of mixed poi in the center for dipping.

NOTE: It is amazing how much like lomi salmon this dip will taste inspite of looking completely different. Poi is a very good dip. Who would have thought that it could be used like this? The only thing missing is the green onion.

VERY BEST HOT BEAN DIP

1 10½-oz. can Jalapeno Bean Dip
8-oz. sour cream
8-oz. cream cheese, softened
½ pkg. taco seasoning mix
⅛ tsp. Tabasco
3 oz. Monterey Jack cheese, grated
3-oz. Cheddar cheese, grated
1 ripe avocado, diced
1 medium tomato, diced and drained
¼ cup green pepper, diced
½ cup black olives, sliced (optional)
Tortilla chips

Mix first 5 incredients and spread in a baking dish. Top with grated cheeses.

Bake at 350° for 15-20 minutes until heated through. Remove from oven.

Top with avocado, tomatoes, green pepper and olives. Dip with regular tortilla chips.

NOTE: Serve with a spoon to be used for scooping up this delicious dip on the tortilla chips. It is not soft like most dips so the chips tend to break. A spoon will come in handy. Most adults love this South of the Border dip.

Vegetables

CUCUMBER CHICKEN RINGS

2 cucumbers
1 large chicken breast, cooked boned and minced
1 hard boiled egg, finely chopped
2 Tbsps. chopped fresh parsley
Salt and pepper to taste
2-3 Tablespoons mayonnaise
Fresh bread
Parsley for garnish

Remove strips of skin from cucumber and cut into thirds. Remove seed, leaving a hole in the center.

Mix minced chicken, chopped egg, parsley, salt and pepper and mayonnaise. Stuff cucumber with this mixture. Wrap in plastic wrap and chill 2-3 hours.

Using a cookie cutter, cut 26 rounds of bread and spread with mayonnaise. Slice cucumbers into ¼-inch slices and place on bread rounds. Serve.

NOTE: If you like crisp cucumbers, soak in iced water for 30 minutes, drain well and stuff. Cucumbers will get soggy if leftover so assemble only what you will need for one sitting. Make more as you need them. Top a few slices with a dash of paprika for color.

CUCUMBER AND WALNUT MISO

⅔ cup walnuts
½ cup red miso
¼ cup sugar
¼ cup mirin
2 Tbsps. rice wine
1 English cucumber

Mince walnuts. In saucepan combine miso, sugar, mirin and rice wine. Cook over low heat, while stirring constantly for 5 minutes.

Remove from heat and stir in walnuts. Set aside to cool.

Cut cucumbers into 3-inch sections and core. Then cut each section into 1-inch sections and quarter each section. Spoon a little miso and walnut mixture on each section and serve.

NOTE: I would never have dreamed of combining miso and walnuts – not in a million years – and yet, here is a great recipe. Try it and I know you will be pleased and excited about this. It was the hit of our latest New Year's Eve party.

Here, again, cucumbers will get soggy if left sitting so fill only what you need for one sitting.

SOUR CREAM AND CUCUMBERS

2 cucumbers, peeled and thinly sliced
1 small onion, thinly sliced
⅓-½ cup distilled vinegar
Salt and pepper to taste
2 Tbsps. sugar
8 oz. sour cream

Place cucumbers and onions in shallow dish. Cover with vinegar, salt, pepper and sugar. Chill overnight. Next day, drain well, mix in sour cream and adjust taste. Chill until ready to serve.

DAY AHEAD VEGETABLES

4-oz. Hidden Valley Ranch original salad dressing mix
1 cup mayonnaise
1 cup sour cream
2 green onions, green parts only chopped
1 lb. bite-size broccoli flowerets
1 lb. bite-size cauliflower flowerets
3 carrots, peeled, sliced ¼" thick

The day before serving prepare vegetables. With wire whisk mix dressing mix with sour cream and mayonnaise. Add chopped green onions and pour over vegetables. Place in ziplock plastic bag, remove all the air and marinate overnight, turning occasionally.

EGG ROLLS WITH PEANUT BUTTER

1½ cups beansprouts
1 cup cooked shrimp, diced
1 cup cooked beef, minced, or raw ground beef
1 cup celery, minced
1 cup green onion, finely minced
1 6½-oz. can water chestnuts, drained and diced
1 Tbsp. oil
4 Tbsps. creamy peanut butter
1½ tsps. salt
1½ tsps. sugar
⅛ tsp. ground black pepper
¼ tsp. Chinese 5 spice powder
20-21 egg roll wrappers

Mix all ingredients except egg roll wrappers.

Place 2-3 teaspoons of mixture in center of egg roll wrappers. Fold both sides toward the center and roll. Moisten end to seal. Fry in lots of hot oil until gold brown in color.

Serve with hot mustard mixed with shoyu or a sweet sour sauce for dipping.

NOTE: The peanut butter gives a nice, different flavor to an otherwise ordinary egg roll. Add more if you are partial to peanut butter when you try it the second time, as I know you will.

KOREAN OGO (SEAWEED)

2 lbs. ogo (seaweed)
½ cup rice vinegar
¾ cup shoyu
⅓ cup sugar
1 tsp. hot sauce
6 stalks green onion, chopped
1 small onion, sliced thin
½ tsp. grated ginger
1 clove garlic, grated
2 Tbsps. dried shrimps, chopped
1 small Hawaiian chili pepper, seeded and chopped

Clean and wash ogo. Boil water in a medium saucepan and add ogo, stir briskly for a few seconds until ogo turns green.

Pour into a colander and rinse under running water to stop cooking process. Drain.

Make marinade with remaining ingredients. Add chopped, drained ogo and mix well. Taste, add more seasoning if desired. Marinate in the refrigerator overnight and serve.

NOTE: This recipe makes enough sauce to amply marinate 2 pounds of ogo. I changed the quantities of the ingredients from the original recipe I found in a local cookbook many years ago. It is always a hit, no matter how many times I serve it.

LUMPIA WITH LETTUCE AND SLIGHTLY SOUR APRICOT SAUCE

6-oz. cooked frozen baby shrimps, thawed
1 Tbsp. vegetable oil
¼ lb. fresh pork sausage
1 clove garlic, minced
1 medium onion, diced
2 cups Chinese cabbage, minced
1 cup fresh beansprouts
¼ tsp. salt
¼ tsp. black pepper
20-24 firm lettuce leaves
Slightly Sour Apricot Sauce

Drain shrimps, set aside. Heat oil in large skillet. Add sausage, garlic and onion, sauté 10 minutes until sausage is completely cooked. Add Chinese cabbage, beansprouts, salt and pepper. Cook 3-5 minutes until vegetables are tender-crisp. Stir in shrimp and heat through. Keep warm. Wash lettuce and pat dry. Steam for 30 seconds, then arrange leaves on large serving platter. Divide mixture among leaves and bring sides of each leaf to center, then roll up. Place seam side down and serve warm or at room temperature with Slightly Sour Apricot Sauce.

SLIGHTLY SOUR APRICOT SAUCE

½ cup apricot preserves
¼ cup white wine vinegar
1 tsp. minced ginger
1 Tbsp. honey

Combine above in small saucepan, bring to a boil. Cool and serve.

OCCIDENTAL NAMASU

3 large cucumbers
3 medium cauliflowers
2 medium daikons (white radish)
4 medium carrots
8-10 stalks celery
4 large sweet onions
2 cups sugar
1½ cups water
1 cup distilled vinegar
¼ cup Hawaiian (rock) salt

Cut cucumbers into 2½-inch Julienne strips, leaving skin but removing seeds. Do the same with the daikon, carrots and celery. Cut cauliflowers into bite-sized pieces. Cut each onion into 8 quarters.

Mix remaining ingredients and pour over cut vegetables in a large bowl. Mix well, cover with saran to keep it from drying out and refrigerate for 2 days, turning frequently. Yields about 2 gallons.

NOTE: Don't worry that the sauce doesn't cover the vegetables. Water will come out of the vegetables as they marinate. This recipe makes a large quantity and is good for receptions and fund-raisers. Do not use an aluminum bowl when marinating the vegetables.

SAUERKRAUT BALLS

½ lb. pork sausage, finely crumbled
¼ cup onion, finely chopped
1 14-oz. can sauerkraut, drained and chopped
2 Tbsps. bread crumbs
3 oz. cream cheese
2 Tbsps. parsley, chopped
1 tsp. prepared mustard
¼ tsp. garlic salt
⅛ tsp. pepper
¼ cup flour
1 egg, well beaten
¼ cup milk
¾ cup bread crumbs

In medium frying pan, brown sausage and onions. Drain fat and add sauerkraut and 2 tablespoons bread crumbs. Combine cream cheese, parsley, mustard, garlic salt and pepper and stir into meat mixture and chill. Shape into small balls after 2 hours and coat with flour. Dip into mixture of egg and milk and then into bread crumbs. Fry in hot oil until lightly browned, about 3-5 minutes.

NOTE: This may be prepared a day ahead, refrigerated and warmed in the oven before serving. Will keep well in the refrigerator for several days. I love sauerkraut so I was happy to find this pupu recipe.

SHIOFUKE KONBU WARABE

1-1½ lbs. warabe (fern shoot)
1 1.5-oz. pkg. shiofuke konbu (salted seaweed slivers), chopped
1 kamabuko, slivered
1 small round onion, sliced thin
Handful dried shrimp, chopped
½-1 tsp. sesame oil

Clean warabe in water, washing off all the hair, dirt, etc. Break off woody, brittle ends. Cut into 1½-inch pieces. Boil a large pot of water. Have a large bowl of water with ice sitting on the side. Place cut warabe in boiling water, stir and blanch for about 30 seconds or until warabe turns bright green. Drain immediately and place warabe in bowl of ice water to stop cooking process. Drain warabe when ice has completely melted. Place warabe in bowl with shiofuke konbu, sliced onions, chopped shrimp, slivered kamabuko and sesame oil. Mix well and refrigerate for an hour or two until ready to eat.

NOTE: The secret to the crunchiness of this recipe is the ice-water bath. For variation mix cooked warabe with sliced tomatoes and use namasu sauce as a marinade. I've also enjoyed warabe with chopped, salted salmon as the only source of seasoning with some chopped round onion. It was very delicious and refreshing. Good as a salad or vegetable dish.

SPINACH BALLS

½ cup butter
2 large onions, chopped
2 boxes frozen chopped spinach
6 eggs
1 tsp. seasoned salt
2 cups Pepperidge farm herbed stuffing
1 cup grated Parmesan cheese
½ tsp. thyme
1 tsp. pepper
1 tsp. garlic salt

Melt butter in skillet, saute onions. Defrost & squeeze-dry spinach. Add to onion and cook 1-2 minutes. Combine eggs, seasoned salt, stuffing, cheese and seasonings. Add spinach mixture. Shape into 1" balls. Place on foil-lined cookie sheet and bake at 350° for 20 minutes until golden.

NOTE: Spinach balls may be frozen on cookie sheets, then wrapped airtight.

SPINACH QUICHE SQUARES

1 cup milk
1 cup flour
3 eggs, beaten
½ tsp. baking powder
1 clove garlic, finely chopped
1 lb. white Monterey Jack cheese, shredded
4 10-oz. packages frozen spinach, thawed and drained
¼ cup butter

In a large bowl mix well the first 5 ingredients. Add cheese and spinach. Melt the butter in a 9x12-inch baking pan while oven is preheating at 350°, approximately 3-4 minutes. Pour spinach mixture into pan into all corners.

Bake at 350° for 30 minutes or until edges are browned. Cool completely and cut into 1½-inch squares. You can quick-freeze them at this point, drop them into a plastic bag and store in the freezer.

To serve, heat in 350° oven for 15 minutes without defrosting.

NOTE: Tastes almost like the Artichoke Nibbles from Pupus: Island Adaptations and just as delicious.

SPINACH TORTILLA ROLL

2 10-oz. pkgs. frozen chopped spinach, drained
1 2-oz. pkg. Hidden Valley Ranch dressing mix
8 oz. sour cream
1 cup mayonnaise
½ of 3.4 oz. bottle bacon bits
¼ cup water chestnuts, chopped
6 stalks green onion, chopped
8 flour tortillas

Thaw and drain frozen spinach, squeeze excess liquid and chop fine. Add remaining ingredients and mix well.

Place ⅓ cup of mixture on a tortilla and spread evenly over the entire surface. Roll as you would sushi and set aside, seam side down, until you have finished rolling all the spinach mixture.

Chill until time to serve. Cut into ¼-inch slices and serve.

NOTE: I have used this as a sandwich spread on whole wheat bread and have had people rave about it. It is especially nice double-deckered and cut into tea-size sandwiches. I have also used this as a vegetable dip, using more mayonnaise to make it more dippable.

STUFFED CHERRY TOMATOES

20-25 cherry tomatoes
¾ cup pitted, imported oil-cured olives
4 anchovy filets
1 clove garlic
2 Tbsps. well-drained capers
1 Tbsp. fresh basil, chopped
1 Tbsp. fresh parsley, chopped
1 Tbsp. lemon juice
3 Tbsps. olive oil

Cut tops off cherry tomatoes. Seed and turn upside down on a paper towel-lined plate. Coarsely chop olives and set aside. Rinse anchovies in cold water and pat dry.

In blender or processor with steel blade, combine olives, anchovies, garlic, capers, basil, parsley and lemon juice. Process until finely minced. Slowly add olive oil. Remove mixture to a bowl and stir well.

Pack each cherry tomato with about 1½ teaspoons of olive mixture. Set on parsley or lettuce-lined plate. Serve at room temperature.

NOTE: Do not freeze. Fill tomatoes an hour before serving. Filling may be made a day or more ahead and kept refrigerated. Bring to room temperature before serving. This has an exotic taste and is very delicious. Wash anchovy well as it is very salty.

SWEET AND SOUR MARINATED ONIONS

3½ Tbsps. olive oil
1 small onion, chopped
1 clove garlic, minced
1 medium tomato, skinned and chopped
1 sprig parsley
1 bay leaf
¼ tsp. basil
¼ tsp. thyme
½ tsp. salt
White pepper to taste
½ lb. pearl onions, 1½ inches in diameter, peeled
¼ cup white wine vinegar
2 Tbsps. raisins
2 tsps. sugar

Heat 2 tablespoons oil in small skillet and sauté chopped onion and garlic until onion is wilted. Add tomato, sauté for a minute, then add the parsley, bay leaf, ⅛ teaspoon of basil and thyme, salt, pepper and 2 tablespoons of water. Cover and simmer for 20 minutes. Place the pearl onions in a saucepan with ½ cup water, vinegar, the remaining 1½ tablespoons of oil, the tomato mixture, the remaining ⅛ teaspoon of basil and thyme, the raisins, salt, pepper and sugar. Bring to a boil, reduce to a simmer and cook uncovered for 45 minutes. Cool and refrigerate. The onions will keep for many days in the refrigerator.

NOTE: Using only onions as a pupu is unusual but you will enjoy this once you try it.

Chicken

BAKED CHICKEN WINGS

¾ cup grated Parmesan cheese
1½ tsps. parsley, chopped
¾ cup herb-seasoned bread crumbs
1½ tsps. garlic salt
16 wings, split at joints
½ cup melted butter

Combine cheese, parsley, bread crumbs and garlic salt.

Dip wings in butter and roll in crumb mixture.

Bake at 350° for 18 minutes or at 450° for 15 minutes. Serve warm or cold.

NOTE: This recipe is one that is both simple and fast but with good results. You will notice other recipes using grated Parmesan cheese as a coating. It has a nice flavor and texture.

Make bread crumbs by blenderizing herb-seasoned stuffing mix. Here again I had to improvise and came up with the idea of using the stuffing mix rather than mixing herbs and bread crumbs. So, do the same, improvise as you go along and you will be pleased with the results. After all, a recipe is only the basics from which you can branch out as far as your imagination will take you.

BUTTERED-HONEY CHICKEN BITS

4 chicken breasts, boned
4 Tbsps. butter
4 Tbsps. honey
2 tsps. teriyaki sauce
1 tsp. salt
½ tsp. garlic salt
¼ tsp. pepper
½ cup sesame seeds

Melt butter and honey in small saucepan. Add teriyaki sauce.

Sprinkle bite-sized pieces of chicken breast with salt, garlic salt and pepper.

Dip each piece into honey, butter and teriyaki sauce mixture and roll in sesame seeds.

Place chicken pieces on baking sheet. Bake at 350° for about 30 minutes, turning once to brown evenly. Reheat remaining sauce to serve with cooked pieces of chicken.

NOTE: Mix 1 Tbsp. cornstarch and ¼ cup water. Add just enough of this mixture to remaining sauce to thicken and use as a dip.

Freezes well. The sesame seeds will fall off but just pile them on again when reheating in the oven before serving.

CHICKEN WINGS STUFFED WITH CREAM CHEESE

2½ lbs. (about 16) large chicken wings

1 Tbsp. rice wine
3 Tbsps. light shoyu

Stuffing:
6 oz. cream cheese
2 Tbsps. chopped fresh ginger
3 Tbsps. chopped scallion
2 Tbsps. fresh coriander
1 Tbsp. light shoyu
2 tsps. sesame oil

To bone chicken wings, cut to the bone above the joint joining the wing to the wing drummet. Grab the joint with a paper towel to keep your hand from slipping and twist; the bone of the drummet should come out. Push the meat up, exposing most of the bone. With your finger, make a small pocket where the bone was lodged.

Repeat the procedure for the joint between the wing and wing tip. Bone all the wings. Marinate the wings in rice wine and shoyu for 1 hours in the refrigerator.

Preheat oven to 500°. In small bowl mix together cream cheese stuffing ingredients. Stuff about 1 teaspoon in each wing using a small spoon or your fingers.

Line the stuffed wings in a baking pan, skin side up. Reduce oven temperature to 400° and bake wings for about 20 minutes, until golden brown.

NOTE: This is worth the bother of boning the wings. Follow the directions and things will work out.

CABBAGE ROLLS

1 whole Chinese cabbage
1 Tbsp. cornstarch
¾ cup diced chicken breast
¼ cup bamboo shoots, diced
1 Tbsp. green peas
2 tsps. light shoyu
1 tsp. sesame oil
Pinch of salt and white pepper

Remove core from cabbage and remove 8 best leaves. Parboil until soft enough for easy rolling; not too soft. Drain and pat dry with paper towels. Sprinkle evenly with cornstarch on both sides of the leaves. Combine remaining ingredients. Divide into 8 balls. Place one ball on each of the 8 leaves. Roll into little envelopes. Steam rolls on high heat for 15 minutes. Slice and serve.

CHICKEN LOAF

1 lb. chicken thighs
4 dried Shiitake mushrooms, soaked in warm water until soft, then minced
½ cup scallions, minced
⅓ cup carrots, minced
2 tsps. fresh ginger juice
2 eggs
1 cup Japanese-style breadcrumbs
4 tsps. miso
2 Tbsps. rice wine (sake)
Oil

Bone chicken thighs; mince the meat fine. Do not use food processor; meat may lose its texture. Add all remaining ingredients except oil and mix well until texture is paste-like.

Brush oil on a cookie sheet with edges. Spread mixture evenly about ⅓-inch thick. Preheat oven at 400°. Bake on center shelf for 15 minutes. Move the sheet to the top shelf and turn heat up to broil. Broil for 2 minutes or until the top is golden brown. Take care that the fat from the chicken does not catch on fire. (If it does, keep oven door closed until it burns itself out. Do not open the door as oxygen will feed the fire.)

Remove from the oven and lift the loaf onto a double thickness of paper towels to drain excess fat. Cut into 1x1½-inch rectangles while hot. Cool and serve at room temperature.

NOTE: This freezes well after broiling. Thaw and serve.

CHICKEN WING CRISPS

3 lbs. chicken wings
⅓ cup white wine
⅔ cup corn oil
1 pkg. (0.7-oz.) Good Seasons Garlic Salad Dressing Mix

Cut off wing tips and discard, cutting remainder in half. Place in Pyrex baking dish. Combine wine, oil and dressing mix, pour over wing sections and marinate several hours in the refrigerator.

Place in a large baking pan, bake in 325° oven for 15-20 minutes. Turn and brush with marinade and bake 15-20 minutes longer.

Broil on both sides until crispy before serving.

NOTE: Wings can be prepared up to the point of broiling the day before and refrigerated until time to broil and serve. They can also be frozen if prepared days ahead, thawed and broiled just before serving.

This keeps well in the freezer so freeze leftovers for unexpected company. You will be known as a most gracious and willing hostess.

MACADAMIA CHICKEN STRIPS

2 cups flour
1-2 tsps. salt, depending on saltiness of nuts
12 oz. roasted macadamia nuts, finely chopped
1 lb. chicken, boned, cut in strips ¾x3-inches long
½ cup butter, melted
4 eggs, lightly beaten

Preheat oven to 350°. Pour flour and salt into a plastic bag. Place nuts into another plastic bag. Taking a small handful at a time, dip chicken strips in melted butter to coat, then flour-filled bag. Shake to coat and shake off excess flour from chicken. Dip in beaten eggs. Shake off excess egg and place in macadamia nut-filled bag. Shake to coat. Place chicken strips on ungreased, non-stick cookie sheet and bake 20 minutes.

NOTE: Store in refrigerator in an airtight container if done ahead, serve at room temperature.

This can also be frozen. Thaw and serve at room temperature or warm in oven before serving.

I love pecans so I used chopped pecans in place of the macadamia and it was also very good. So, once again, use whatever is your pleasure.

MINI-CHICKEN FILO ROLLS

1 chicken breast, finely minced
8 water chestnuts, finely minced
1 4-oz. can mushrooms, finely minced
2 stalks green onion, finely minced
1 Tbsp. cornstarch
1 tsp. sesame oil
1 tsp. light shoyu
½ tsp. distilled vinegar
½ tsp. sugar
½ tsp. salt
½ tsp. Sherry
1 tsp. oyster sauce
1 Tbsp. ginger, finely minced
9 sheets filo dough
1 beaten egg
4 cups oil

Mix all ingredients except last 3, let stand overnight in refrigerator. Cut filo sheets lengthwise into 4 equal strips. Brush 1 strip with a little oil, using your fingers, and lay another strip on top. Brush second strip with same amount of oil. Place 1 tablespoon filling on one end of strip, shaping filling into a cylinder. Roll filling up once, then fold left and right side of strip ½-inch lengthwise to enclose the filling. Continue rolling filo all the way to the end. Seal with beaten egg. Repeat procedure with rest of filo and filling. Heat oil in wok over medium high heat. Deep fry chicken rolls until golden. Drain on paper towel. Cool slightly before serving.

MOCK CHICKEN LEGS

1 cup plum wine
¼ cup shoyu
¼ cup molasses
2 Tbsps. wine vinegar
2 scallions (green onion), minced
2 cloves garlic, minced
1 Tbsp. grated ginger
40 chicken wings (3½ lbs.)
Garlic-Soy Dipping Sauce

Combine wine, shoyu, molasses, vinegar, scallions, garlic and ginger in mixing bowl and set aside.

Cut off the tips and middle* portions of the wings. Reserve for use later as stock, etc. With a sharp knife, loosen the meat around the middle joint and push the meat down gently, scraping the bone to about three-fourths of the length. Turn the meat inside out around the big joint to form a drumstick.

Marinate the chicken wings for 4 hours or overnight in the refrigerator.

Grill the wing "legs" over hot coals or in a broiler until golden brown. Serve with Garlic-Soy Dipping Sauce that follows.

NOTE: *The middle portion of the wings may be used as with drumette section by discarding one of the two bones. Push the meat down and turn it inside out to form a mini-drumstick.

GARLIC-SOY DIPPING SAUCE

4 Tbsps. shoyu
3 Tbsps. rice wine vinegar
2 Tbsps. vegetable oil
Pinch of sugar
1 tsp. sesame oil
1 tsp. garlic, minced
1 tsp. scallion, minced

Mix all the ingredients shortly before serving.

Serve as a dipping sauce for won ton, dumplings, meatballs, etc.

Makes 1 cup which is enough for the preceding recipe. But this is good enough to be made in a larger quantity and stored in the refrigerator to be used with other every-day type of cooking. Just a little bit added to stir-fry dishes is very good for a slightly different flavor from most stir-fry dishes.

SPINACH-WRAPPED CHICKEN WITH ORIENTAL DIP

2 lbs. chicken breasts
1 14-oz. can chicken broth
¼ cup shoyu
1 Tbsp. Pickapeppa
1 lb. fresh spinach
Oriental Dip

Place chicken breasts in broth, shoyu and Pickapeppa in pan and bring to a boil. Simmer 15-20 minutes until fork tender. Lift chicken from broth, cool. Remove and discard skin and bones then cut meat into 1-inch chunks. Wash spinach, remove and discard stems and parboil. Drain thoroughly; set aside to cool. Place chunk of chicken at stem end of a large spinach leaf. Roll over once, fold leaf in toward center on both sides and continue rolling and secure with toothpick. Refrigerate finished spinach rolls until thoroughly chilled or until the next day. Serve cold with Oriental Dip that follows. Yield: 50-60 pieces.

ORIENTAL DIP

Stir together ½ cup sour cream, 1 tsp. toasted sesame seed, ¼ tsp. ground ginger, 2 tsps. shoyu and 1 tsp. Worcestershire sauce until blended. Refrigerate until chilled or until the next day.

SWEET-SOUR (BARBECUE) CHICKEN WINGS

40 chicken wings
1 14-oz. bottle catsup
1 8-oz. can tomato sauce
1 cup cider vinegar
Dash of Worcestershire sauce
1 tsp. dry (Coleman) mustard
1 tsp. ground ginger
1 cup brown sugar
1 cup white sugar

Cut off and discard wing tips. Cut wings at joint and place in rectangular baking dish in a single layer. Mix remaining ingredients and pour over wings, turning them once to coat completely. Bake, uncovered at 350° for 2 hours, turning several times, until sugar cooks down and wings are well glazed. Be certain to have enough sauce to cover the wings before baking.

NOTE: If the quantity of sauce is insufficient to cover the wings, make another half-recipe to completely cover the wings. This is a Texas-style barbecue sauce and good with shortribs, spare ribs, etc. It is a nice change from the usual teriyaki-style chicken we serve so often.

These wings will disappear in no time and I don't mean flying away!!!

Meats

BARBECUED BEEF STRIPS

2 lbs. flank steak
1 medium yellow onion, peeled and thinly sliced
2 bay leaves, crushed
10 whole black peppercorns
1 cup Marsala (wine)
2 cloves garlic, minced
¼ tsp. white pepper
3 Tbsps. brown sugar
¼ cup shoyu
⅓ cup olive oil
1 small bunch Chinese parsley
3-4 sprigs thyme

Cut steak crosswise at 45° angle to make strips 1"x⅛"x5-6" wide. Set aside.

Combine remaining ingredients in large mixing bowl, add meat strips and marinate overnight in the refrigerator.

Weave 5" skewer into each strip and grill 4-5 minutes, turning once.

BARBECUED BRISKET ON BUNS

3 lbs. brisket of beef
1 cup catsup
1 tsp. salt
2 cups water
⅓ cup Worcestershire Sauce
½ tsp. Tabasco
1 tsp. chili powder
1 tsp. liquid smoke
1 small onion, chopped
½ cup brown sugar

Cook brisket, uncovered, in a 350° oven for 2 hours. Mix remaining ingredients; pour over the meat and cook, covered, another 2 hours at 300°

Cover and refrigerate meat and sauce overnight in the refrigerator.

The next day, slice the meat paper-thin; lay them in a flat pan overlapping, cover with the sauce and heat in a 300° oven. Serve with dinner rolls or buns.

NOTE: When a recipe calls for a baking pan to be covered in the oven, use heavy-duty foil and crimp the edges securely. This will keep the heat within the pan and the end result is a softer, juicier roast. This is also good enough to be used as a luncheon dish.

BEEF SASHIMI

2 lbs. Filet of beef

Marinade:
2 round onions, thinly sliced
2 cloves garlic, thinly sliced
4 thin slices of lemon
½ cup plus 2 Tbsps. rice vinegar
½ cup shoyu
¼ cup rice wine (sake)

Barbecue on charcoal or broil in the oven the filet approximately 4 minutes on one side and 3 minutes on the other. DO NOT OVERCOOK. Plunge beef in ice water to stop cooking process and wash off any burned parts. Pat dry and set aside.

Combine all marinade ingredients in a large plastic bag. Place the filet in the bag and seal, removing all air from the bag. This will eliminate having to turn the meat periodically. Refrigerate for 24 to 36 hours.

Remove the filet from the marinade, slice thin against the grain and serve at room temperature. The inside should be medium-rare.

NOTE: This is a very tasty and completely different way to serve beef. Use lean tenderloin, broil off the fat and you need not worry about cholesterol. Just remember that the filet must be marinated 2 to 3 days, whichever is your preference, so do plan ahead. You will be well rewarded for your efforts.

BURRITOS

1 lb. ground beef
1 bell pepper, chopped
1 whole green chili, seeded and chopped
1-2 stalks celery, chopped
¼ tsp. pepper
¾ tsp. salt
½ tsp. oregano
½ tsp. coriander
2 cloves garlic, chopped
15-oz. can Hormel chili, no beans
16-oz. can Rosarita refried beans
24 6-inch flour tortillas

Brown meat in saucepan. Add next 8 ingredients with ¼ cup water and simmer 1½ hours until tender. Add more water if necessary to prevent burning. Drain excess liquid when cooked.

Add chili and refried beans. Mix well. Place heaping tablespoonful on a tortilla, roll once, fold in both edges and continue rolling. Place seam-side down in a baking dish and bake for 40 minutes in a 250° oven.

NOTE: There was some filling leftover so I wrapped it in won ton pi and fried it. It was simply delicious!! Be certain to seal the pi completely so filling will not spill out and splatter in the hot oil. Cook over medium heat so it will be nicely browned and crisp. Enjoy!! One cup of filling made 20 burrito won tons.

CHINESE ROAST PORK STRIPS

1 lb. pork tenderloin
3 Tbsps. shoyu
2 Tbsps. Hoisin sauce
2 Tbsps. Sherry
1 Tbsp. brown sugar
1 clove garlic, crushed

Mix shoyu, Hoisin sauce, Sherry, brown sugar and garlic. Marinate pork for 4 hours or overnight.

Place meat on a rack in a roasting pan. Pour ½" water into roasting pan. Bake at 300° for 1½ hours.

Cut tenderloin into ½" strips and serve with toothpicks. Serve with Sweet and Sour Dipping Sauce.

SWEET AND SOUR DIPPING SAUCE

1 cup peach preserves
½ cup mango chutney
2 Tbsps. lemon juice
2 Tbsps. water

Place ingredients in a food processor and blend until smooth.

NOTE: This is a delicious sauce which is very versatile. Use it as a dipping sauce for all meats and poultry. You will love it.

DRIED BEEF CHUNKS

1½ lbs. boneless beef shoulder
2 Tbsps. corn oil
2 Tbsps. sugar
¾ to 1 cup water
1 tsp. shallots, chopped*
1 Tbsp. Galliano
¼ to ½ tsp. cayenne pepper
½ tsp. salt
2 Tbsps shoyu
Garlic salt

Preheat oven to 200°. Cut beef into ¾-inch cubes, trimming off all fat. Heat oil in frying pan, add sugar and beef cubes. Sear and sugar-coat the beef for 4-5 minutes. Stir in remaining ingredients except garlic salt. Bring to a boil then reduce heat to medium. Cover and cook 30 minutes, stirring frequently. During the last 5 minutes, remove cover and let most of liquid evaporate. Transfer beef to a baking sheet and lightly sprinkle with garlic salt. Reduce oven to 175° and dry beef for approximately 45 minutes. Turn off heat and let beef cubes cool in the oven. Store in a covered container in the refrigerator. Will keep for days in the refrigerator.

*Shallots look like miniature, elongated round onions with a strong onion flavor. Use round onion if unable to find shallots.

NOTE: This freezes very well. Thaw to room temperature and serve with colored food picks. Garnish with parsley sprigs.

GLAZED SAUSAGE BALLS

⅓ lb. pork sausage
¾ lb. ground pork or beef
½ tsp. salt
½ tsp. dry mustard
½ tsp. coriander seeds (crushed)
¼ tsp. ground allspice
1 egg, lightly beaten
¼ cup fine dry bread crumbs
¼ cup thinly sliced green onion
½ cup apple jelly
½ cup chutney, finely chopped
1 tsp. lemon juice

In a bowl stir together sausage, ground pork, salt, mustard, coriander, allspice, egg, bread crumbs and onion until well blended. Shape into 1-inch balls. (May be refrigerated or frozen at this point.)

Place meatballs (thaw if frozen) on rimmed baking sheet and bake uncovered at 500° for about 8 minutes or until well browned; drain.

In large frying pan over low heat, stir together apple jelly, chutney and lemon juice; cook, stirring, until jelly is melted. Add meatballs; then cover and simmer for another 8 to 10 minutes or until glazed. Transfer to a chafing dish to keep warm and serve warm.

NOTE: The rimmed baking sheet will keep oil from spilling over the edge and possibly causing an oven fire.

GRILLED SIRLOIN WITH SESAME

1 Tbsp. sesame seeds
1 Tbsp. sesame oil
1 tsp. ginger, minced
1 clove garlic, minced
1 scallion, both white and green parts, minced
1-2 Tbsps. honey
¾ cup shoyu
Freshly ground pepper
2 lbs. boneless sirloin, cut in 2-inch strips

Toast sesame seeds over low heat in frying pan, stirring constantly until golden. Remove from frying pan and combine with sesame oil, ginger, garlic, scallions, honey to taste, shoyu and pepper to taste.

Add sirloin to shoyu mixture and marinate for at least 2 hours in the refrigerator. While marinating sirloin pieces, soak bamboo skewers in cold water to prevent it from burning.

Skewer one or two pieces, spaced slightly apart, and grill until partially done. Do not overcook pieces as they will become dry.

Garnish plate with parsley, place grilled sirloin skewers on it and serve.

PORK SAUSAGE CHEESE BALLS

1 lb. Hoffy pork sausage
1 cup Bisquick
6 oz. grated Cheddar cheese
¼ cup chopped round onion

Combine above ingredients with hands. Form into quarter-sized balls and bake at 350° on a cookie sheet for 15-20 minutes until slightly golden.

NOTE: This freezes well. For variations, use ground round or ground chicken or turkey. When using turkey, you will need to add some seasoning to your taste.

HOT DOG BACON WRAP

1½ lbs. hot dogs, cut in thirds
1 lb. bacon, cut in thirds
½ cup catsup
2 Tbsps. brown sugar
2 Tbsps. cider vinegar
1 Tbsp. soy sauce
1 Tbsp. Worcestershire sauce
½ tsp. prepared (hot dog) mustard

Wrap hot dogs with bacon and pin with toothpick. Lay in single layer in baking pan. Mix remaining ingredients and pour over hot dogs. Bake for 30-35 minutes at 350°, turning once.

HOISIN SAUCE BABY RIBS

2 cloves garlic, minced
1 Tbsp. ginger, grated
2 tsps. horseradish sauce
1¼ tsp. cayenne pepper
3 Tbsps. brown sugar
¼ cup molasses
½ cup hoisin sauce
½ cup dark soy sauce
½ cup red currant jelly
30 small pork ribs, trimmed of fat

Mix together all the marinade ingredients. Pour over the ribs in a plastic bag, remove all the air, seal and marinate in the refrigerator overnight.

Preheat oven to 375°. Put ribs on a rack over a foil-lined baking sheet. Bake, turning often and basting with the remaining marinade until the ribs are a dark, golden brown, approximately 30-35 minutes. Serve hot or warm. Cut into one rib to see that it is cooked.

NOTE: This is simply delicious and simple to do. Hoisin sauce and dark soy sauce are available in the Oriental section at most markets. Any red jelly will do if you cannot find currant (grape) jelly.

MEATBALLS WITH GRAPE JELLY

1 lb. ground beef
1 egg
2 Tbsps. bread crumbs
Salt, pepper, onion salt and garlic salt to taste

Mix above ingredients and shape into balls smaller than walnuts. Set aside.

1 12-oz. bottle of ketchup
1 6-oz. jar grape jelly
Juice from 1 lemon

Mix above ingredients and melt in heavy skillet.

Place meatballs in rows in the skillet and cook covered for 30 minutes and another 15 minutes uncovered.

Remove meatballs to a covered bowl and refrigerate. Freeze sauce so you can easily remove grease that floats to the surface. When ready to serve, heat sauce once again, add meatballs. warm and serve.

NOTE: The sauce is just great. For cholesterol-watchers, use ground turkey and egg substitute.

SWEDISH MEATBALLS

½ cup fine, dry breadcrumbs
1 cup light cream, warm
½ lb. ground beef
½ lb. ground veal
½ lb. ground pork
2 egg yolks, slightly beaten
2 Tbsps. onions, finely chopped
1½ tsps. salt
¼ tsp. pepper
½ tsp. sugar
3 Tbsps. butter, melted

Soak crumbs in warmed cream for 5 minutes. Add meats and mix well. Add remaining ingredients; mix well and shape into 1-inch balls. Fry meatballs in single layer in preheated 350° oven until evenly browned. Serve with any sweet and sour dipping sauce.

ORIENTAL MEATBALLS

¼ lb. ground pork sausage
¼ lb. cooked shrimp, finely chopped
¼ cup water chestnuts, finely chopped
¼ cup onions, finely chopped
2 Tbsps. shoyu
¼ tsp. sugar
1 egg, slightly beaten

Combine all ingredients in a bowl. Shape into 1-inch balls and fry in pre-heated 350° oven until brown. Serve hot with Chinese hot mustard for dipping.

PIZZA SKINS

3 oz. cream cheese, softened
½ cup butter, softened
1½ cups flour
2 cups instant mashed potatoes
4 strips of bacon, crisped
1 cup Cheddar cheese, grated

Make crust by beating cheese and butter together. Add flour and blend well. Form dough into a ball, cover with plastic wrap to prevent it from drying out and refrigerate for at least 30 minutes.

Roll dough to fit the bottom and sides of an 8-inch round or 13x4-inch tart pan and bake at 450° for 7-10 minutes or until lightly browned at the edges.

When cooled, fill with mashed potatoes, cover with Cheddar cheese and top with bacon bits. Bake at 350° for 5-7 minutes until cheese is melted. Cut into wedges or squares and serve warm or at room temperature.

NOTE: When crisping bacon, slice into thin slivers and fry until crisp. You will be surprised at how much more you get by doing it in this fashion. Much easier and less messy, too.

Had something like this in Honolulu and the above is the end result.

REUBEN ROLLUPS

4 oz. Swiss cheese, grated
1 cup sauerkraut, very well drained
¼ cup prepared mustard
30 slices pastrami

Combine Swiss cheese with the sauerkraut. Spread a thin layer of mustard on each pastrami slice. Heap a generous spoonful of the cheese-sauerkraut mixture on each slice of pastrami.

Roll the meat tightly and skewer it through the center with a cellophane-tipped toothpick.

Refrigerate until serving time.

NOTE: If you prefer to heat this before serving, remove the cellophane-tipped toothpick, place seam-side down on a baking dish and bake for 5 minutes at 350° and serve immediately after reinserting pick to hold it together.

STIR-FRIED BEEF WITH LETTUCE

4 medium shiitake (Japanese black) mushrooms
1¼ lbs. ground beef
4-oz. bamboo shoots, coarsely minced
2 cloves garlic, finely minced
2 slices ginger, finely minced
4 water chestnuts, coarsely minced
1 stalk scallion (green onion) chopped
4 Tbsps. peanut oil
1 tsp. salt
¼ tsp. pepper
1 Tbsp. light shoyu
½ Tbsp. black bean paste
½ Tbsp. hoisin sauce
½ Tbsp. sugar
1 Tbsp rice wine or dry Sherry
1½ tsps. sesame oil
2 sprigs parsley to garnish
12 lettuce leaves

Remove and discard stems from mushrooms soaked in hot water for 30 minutes. Coarsely mince the caps. Fry beef until browned; drain fat. In hot oil stir-fry ginger and mushrooms for 30 seconds before adding bamboo shoots, garlic and water chestnuts. After 1 minute add scallions and meat together with the salt and pepper. Cook another 2 minutes, stirring continuously. Add the shoyu, bean paste, hoisin sauce, sugar and rice wine and cook another 3 minutes. Add sesame oil and serve garnished with sprigs of parsley. People will help themselves to a couple of spoonfuls of the minced mixture by placing it on a lettuce leaf, wrapping it up carefully and eating it with their fingers.

TOASTED BACON AND CREAM CHEESE ROLLS

1 8-oz. cream cheese
2 Tbsps. cream or milk
12 slices soft white bread
1 pkg. (1 lb.) bacon

Beat together cream cheese and cream with electric mixer.

Remove crusts from bread by stacking and cutting 4 slices at a time. Spread cream cheese mixture on each slice. Cut slices in half, then cut each half into 2 pieces. Also cut bacon into 2½ to 3-inch strips.

Roll each piece of bread jelly roll fashion with filling on the inside. Wrap a piece of bacon around each roll, making sure bacon completely covers the seam so cream cheese will not seep out. Secure with a toothpick.

Before serving, broil until bacon is crisp. Keep on warming tray and serve warm.

NOTE: This can be frozen very nicely after they have been rolled and secured. Thaw and broil as directed above. Do not use cellophane-tipped toothpicks or they will burn while broiling.

UPSIDE-DOWN PIZZA SQUARES

½ lb. raw Italian sausage
½ cup green pepper, chopped
1 small onion, chopped
1 clove garlic, minced
½ tsp. dry basil
½ tsp. thyme leaves
2 Tbsps. butter or margarine
1 cup milk
1½ cups flour
3 eggs
1 14-oz. jar Ragu pizza quick sauce
1 cup Cheddar cheese, shredded

Remove sausage casing, crumble and fry in skillet with next 5 ingredients. Add butter or margarine and when melted, pour mixture into 9x12-inch baking pan. In blender beat eggs with milk and gradually add flour. Pour this carefully over the sausage mixture. Carefully top with pizza sauce, then cheese. Bake at 425° for 15-20 minutes or until topping is puffy and bubbly.

Cut into bite-sized squares when slightly cooled and serve.

NOTE: The original "oven pancake" recipe called for 4 eggs. I eliminated one egg and added ½ cup flour when I tried this the second time. The recipe also called for the pizza sauce to be passed around or spread over the finished "pancake." I tried it as typed above and hope you like the end result.

Seafoods

BACON-WRAPPED SHRIMPS

1 lb. medium-size (30-35 count) shrimps
Boiling water
½ lb. sliced bacon
1 clove garlic, pressed
½ cup tomato-based chili sauce

Cook shrimp in enough boiling water to cover until they turn pink (about 5 minutes). Drain and cool; shell and devein.

Cook bacon strips in frying pan until limp; drain and cut each slice in half crosswise. Stir together garlic and chili sauce until well blended. Dip each shrimp into sauce to coat, wrap in half strip of bacon and secure with a wooden pick. May be refrigerated until the next day at this point.

To cook, place appetizers on a broiler pan and broil 6 inches from broiler unit, turning once, until bacon is crisp (about 5 minutes.) Serve hot.

NOTE: For those who love Shrimp Cocktails, this is a slightly different variation of it. Delicious!!

BAKED IMITATION CRAB

1 lb. imitation crab
½ cub shredded Parmesan cheese
1 cup mayonnaise

Lay imitation crab in 8" baking pan. Cover with mayonnaise over which sprinkle the cheese.

Bake at 350° for 10-15 minutes or until cheese is lightly browned.

NOTE: This can be made into a very nice main dish by simply adding cooked broccoli or asparagus under the crab before baking.

For those who must watch their cholesterol, use Saffola mayonnaise sparingly in place of your regular mayonnaise.

BROILED CRAB AND AVOCADO

3 Tbsps. flour
3 Tbsps. butter
1 cup milk
½ tsp. salt
⅛ tsp. white pepper
¼ cup grated Swiss cheese
¼ cup grated Parmesan cheese
1½ cups cooked shrimp
½ cup meat of King crab legs
4 medium avocados
Lemon juice
Paprika

In medium saucepan, over moderate heat, melt butter and add flour. Stir with whisk until well blended. Cook for 1 minute. Gradually add milk, whisking constantly until smooth and thick. Add seasonings and cheeses and whisk until melted. Add seafood.

Cut avocados in half, leaving skin intact, but removing the pit. Rub inside with lemon juice. Heap seafood mixture onto avocado shells, place on a baking sheet. Dust with paprika. Broil until mixture bubbles. Cut half into quarters or chunks, depending on the consistency of the filling.

NOTE: Island people prefer avocado served cut up rather than halved. You can also remove the skin and cut them in chunks, mix with the crab mixture and bake in a casserole dish at 350° until it bubbles. Serve warm.

BROILED OYSTERS

24 small oysters
1 Tbsp. flour
2 Tbsps onion, finely minced
¼ cup shoyu
1½ Tbsps. rice wine
Oil

Place shucked oysters in bowl, add flour, mix thoroughly to clean. Rinse under cold water and drain.

Mince onion and combine with shoyu and rice wine in a bowl. Add the oysters and coat thoroughly. Set aside to marinate for 15 minutes.

Heat oven broiler. Oil shallow broiling pan lightly and lay oysters out in a single layer. Broil about 4 minutes, turn oysters and broil another 3-4 minutes.

Serve warm or at room temperature.

NOTE: The oysters will have a teriyaki flavor. In the process of broiling, the oysters will shrink so don't be surprised that 24 oysters will yield only a handful or several mouthfuls – so serve sparingly and only to good friends.

If you prefer, this can be coated with flour or breadcrumbs and deep fried.

BROILED VINHA DALHOS SHRIMP

5 lbs. frozen shrimps

2 pkgs. Noh brand Vinha Dalhos powder

Wash shrimp, remove legs if desired, and drain well. Place in a large bowl, add 2 packages of Vinha Dalhos powder and mix well. DO NOT ADD WATER. Refrigerate overnight, turning occasionally.

Broil in a single layer for 3-4 minutes on one side, turning over when shrimp turns slightly pink at the edges and continue broiling for another minute until opaque color is completely gone. DO NOT OVERCOOK.

NOTE: This freezes very well. All you need to do to serve is to thaw to room temperature or warm in the microwave. This is one of the easiest and best pupus. You will be surprised how fast 5 pounds of shrimp will disappear. Keep the shells on as they help retain the flavor and slow down the consumption because it has to be peeled to be eaten.

Variation: You may use cleaned filet of squid or fish. Be certain to score the squid to prevent it from curling when broiling.

CLAM TOAST

1 10-oz. can clams
2 Tbsps. olive oil
1 medium onion, finely chopped
4 Tbsps. parsley, minced
2 cloves garlic, minced
½ dried red chili pepper or
¼ tsp. crushed red pepper
4 tsps. flour
4 slices bread, crust removed, cut in 2 triangles, slightly toasted

Strain liquid from can of clams, reserve ⅓ cup – if less, add bottled clam juice or water. Chop the clams.

Heat oil in skillet and sauté onions slowly until wilted. Cover and continue cooking another 20 minutes until onion is tender. Uncover, turn up heat slightly, add garlic, parsley and chili pepper.

Cook another 2-3 minutes, then stir in flour. Add reserved clam juice and clams and cook over medium-high heat until mixture is thick enough to spread.

Spread on toasted triangles and serve.

NOTE: This can be frozen in a single layer on a cookie sheet and bagged when frozen. To serve, thaw and warm in microwave.

CRABMEAT BALLS

1 cup crabmeat from King Crab legs
3 Tbsps. butter
¼ cup bread crumbs
1 Tbsp. minced onion
3 Tbsps. finely chopped celery
¼ tsp. prepared mustard
1 large egg, beaten
⅛ tsp. paprika
1 tsp. lemon juice
Salt and pepper
Dash of Worcestershire sauce

Melt butter in skillet. Add onion and simmer 3 minutes. Add bread crumbs and stir over heat another 2 minutes. Add other ingredients and mix well.

Form into balls measuring approximately ¾ to 1 inch. Dust your hands with flour or bread crumbs when forming balls. This may be frozen at this stage on a cookie sheet, bagged and stored until ready for use.

Broil 3-5 minutes or until slightly browned.

NOTE: If frozen, thaw balls on the broiler pan and broil until slightly browned.

CRABMEAT PUFF SHELLS

Puff Pastry:
¼ cup shortening
½ cup boiling water
½ cup flour
¼ tsp. salt
2 eggs

On high heat bring water to a boil, add shortening and cook until melted. Add flour and salt, still on high heat, stirring continuously until dough forms a ball and leaves the sides of the pan. Cool 3-4 minutes and beat in eggs, one at a time, beating well after each addition. Drop by ½ teaspoons on greased baking sheet and bake at 400° for 10 minutes. Yields 40-50 puffs.

Filling:
1 cup crabmeat
¼ cup lime juice
3 oz. cream cheese
¼ cup heavy cream
2 Tbsps. mayonnaise
Pinch of salt
1 Tbsp. minced onion
1 clove garlic, minced
1 tsp. finely chopped chives
¼ tsp. Tabasco
1 tsp. Worcestershire sauce

Marinate crabmeat in lime juice for 30 minutes. Whip cream cheese and cream, add remaining ingredients and fold in crabmeat. Fill puffs. Bake at 375° for 10 minutes. Serve warm.

CRABMEAT TOAST

½ lb. meat of King Crab legs
1 tsp. dry Sherry
1 tsp. salt
⅛ tsp. white pepper
1 Tbsp. chopped fresh dill or
  1 tsp. dried dill

1 Tbsp. butter
2 Tbsps. flour
1 egg yolk
1 cup light cream
1 loaf sandwich bread,
  crust trimmed

Combine crabmeat, sherry, salt, pepper and dill in a large mixing bowl and set aside.

Melt butter in a saucepan, remove from heat and stir in flour. In a small bowl beat the egg yolk with cream, then briskly stir into flour/butter roux with wire whisk. Return pan to stove and cook slowly, whisking constantly, for 1-2 minutes or until mixture thickens. Do not let it boil. Pour sauce over crabmeat and stir until well combined.

Toast bread on one side only. Spread untoasted side generously with crabmeat mixture, mounding it slightly. May be prepared in advance up to this point and refrigerated. Place under hot broiler for a minute or so until hot and lightly browned before serving. Cut into fourths and serve.

CURRIED CRAB TRIANGLES

2 Tbsps. onion, chopped
2 Tbsps. butter
¼ cup mushrooms, chopped
¼ tsp. curry powder
½ cup frozen crab leg meat
½ cup mayonnaise
¼ cup grated Parmesan cheese
6 slices bread, crust removed and toasted on one side

Sauté onion and mushrooms in butter. Add curry powder and shredded crab meat. Remove from heat.

Stir in mayonnaise and spread on untoasted side of bread. Sprinkle with cheese and broil until cheese is bubbly.

Cut each square into 4 triangles and serve.

NOTE: This can be frozen before broiling. Lay toast slices in a single layer on a baking sheet and freeze. When frozen, pack in ziplock freezer bag until ready to use.

To serve, partially thaw and broil until done. Cut in triangles and serve.

DEEP-FRIED FISHCAKE ROLLS

1 cup fishcake base
¼ cup water chestnuts, minced
½ cup minced ham or pork
1 Tbsp. green onion, minced
½ tsp. salt
½ tsp. cornstarch
½ tsp. shoyu
½ tsp. liquor

Combine all ingredients and mix well. Divide into two parts and shape into a roll about 1½ inches in diameter. Place on greased pan and steam 15 minutes.

Batter:
1 egg
3 Tbsps. flour
1 Tbsp. water
¼ tsp. salt
Breadcrumbs or cracker meal
Oil for frying

Dip rolls into batter made with egg, flour, water and salt. Roll in breadcrumbs or cracker meal and deep fry until lightly golden. Drain oil. Slice and serve.

NOTE: For variation, wrap in nori before dipping into batter and fry. Rolls can be frozen after steaming. Thaw, dip in batter and fry when ready to use.

GARLIC SHRIMP

3 cloves garlic, crushed in press with skins on
2 dried red chili peppers
1 bay leaf
4 Tbsps. olive oil
1 lb. medium shrimps, unshelled, legs removed, well drained
Salt and pepper to taste

Combine garlic, whole chili peppers, bay leaf and olive oil in a sauté pan and cook over low heat for 2-3 minutes so spices will release their flavor.

Add shrimp and sauté for another 2-3 minutes, turning once, until shrimp is cooked and has lost its opaque color. Do not overcook. Sprinkle with salt and pepper to taste and serve.

NOTE: This freezes very well and is good when planning a large party that requires detailed scheduling. Shrimp freezes beautifully and is enjoyed by almost everyone. Pity the poor person who is allergic to seafood. They miss out on the best of pupus.

LOBSTER SPREAD

2 cups lobster, finely chopped
½ cup mayonnaise
1 Tbsp. A-1 sauce
1 tsp. chopped green onion
½ tsp. lemon juice
Salt and paprika to taste

Mix all above ingredients and serve with wheat thins or other cocktail crackers or bread.

NOTE: This can be served hot by adding ¼ cup mayonnaise and baking at 350° for 20-25 minutes. Good both hot or cold.

OYSTERS PARMESAN

¼ cup olive oil
¼ cup light vegetable oil
2-3 cloves garlic, crushed
1 cup finely grated Parmesan cheese
1 cup finely crushed Ritz crackers
1 pint raw oysters, shucked

Combine oils and garlic in a small bowl. Drain oysters and pat dry with paper towels. Dip oysters into Parmesan cheese, then the oil mixture and finally into cracker crumbs.

Place in a 9" square baking dish and bake at 375° for 15 minutes.

MARINATED BROILED SCALLOPS

2 lbs. medium scallops
½ cup melted butter
1 tsp. garlic salt
3 Tbsps. lemon juice
2 tsps. shoyu
¼ cup Sherry
Paprika
Bread crumbs

Mix together butter, garlic salt, lemon juice and shoyu. Pour over scallops and marinate for one hour. Drain, reserving liquid. Broil scallops until lightly browned. Add Sherry to marinade and spoon over scallops. Sprinkle with bread crumbs and paprika and continue broiling another 1-2 minutes longer.

CHINESE BARBECUED SHRIMP

2 lbs. raw shrimp, shelled and deveined
¾ tsp. salt
Dash of pepper
1 Tbsp. honey
2 Tbsps. shoyu
1 Tbsp. dry Sherry
3 Tbsps. vegetable oil

Place shrimp in a flat baking dish. Combine remaining ingredients, marinate shrimp for 15 minutes. Bake at 375° for 10 minutes.

NOTE: This can be prepared and frozen. Thaw, heat and serve.

ORIENTAL SHRIMP TOAST

3 strips raw bacon
1 lb. raw shrimp, peeled and deveined
½ cup water chestnuts, finely chopped
¼ cup green onion, chopped
2 Tbsps. parsley, chopped
1 tsp. white wine
12 slices white bread, crust removed

With cleaver or sharp knife, mince shrimp and bacon until it forms a paste. Stir in water chestnuts, green onions, parsley and white wine. Spread mixture onto bread. Cover with plastic wrap and refrigerate until ready to deep fry.

Heat oil to 350° . Fry bread with shrimp mixture side down until edges begin to brown. Turn over and cook until lightly browned on all sides. Drain on paper towels, cut each square into 4 triangles with sharp knife and serve hot.

NOTE: Keep Fried Shrimp Toast in 250° oven to keep warm until serving time. It can also be frozen and reheated in 450° oven for about 5-7 minutes but because of our humidity, toast will turn soggy after being out for a while. That's the price of paradise!!

OYSTERS ROCKFELLER

24 oysters in shells
2 Tbsps. onion, chopped
2 Tbsps. butter, melted
2 Tbsps. parsley, chopped
⅛ tsp. paprika
Salt
Pepper
1 cup cooked spinach, chopped fine
¼ cup fine dry bread crumbs
½ cup butter or margarine
Rock salt

If you use shucked oysters, prepare this in small baking shells. Open the oysters with an oyster knife. Remove the oysters from their shells, drain very well. Wash the shells. Place each oyster in the deep half of the shell.

Combine parsley, onion and the melted butter. Spread this over each oyster. Sprinkle each one with a little salt, pepper and paprika. Top each with 2 teaspoons spinach, then ½ teaspoon bread crumbs. Dot each one with about 1 teaspoon of butter. Arrange oyster shells on a bed of rock salt in a shallow pan. The salt will hold the shells upright. Bake at 450° until browned, about 8 to 10 minutes.

SPICY SHRIMP AND BACON KABOBS

1 lb. fresh jumbo shrimps in shells
3 Tbsps. cooking oil
2 Tbsps. Pickapeppa sauce
2 Tbsps. apricot preserves
1 Tbsp. honey
1 Tbsp. maple syrup
1 tsp. crushed red pepper
1 tsp. Szechuan peppercorns, crushed
¼ tsp. dried basil, crushed
¼ tsp. dried oregano, crushed
¼ tsp. dried rosemary, crushed
1 clove garlic, minced
3 Tbsps. lemon juice
7-8 slices bacon

Thaw shrimp, peel and devein. Stir together remaining ingredients except lemon juice and shrimp. Add shrimp, stir, cover and chill for at least 1 hour. Halve bacon slices crosswise. In 10-inch skillet, partially cook bacon. Drain well on paper towels. Drain shrimp, reserving marinade. Wrap each shrimp with a half slice of bacon; thread on 4-inch skewers. Squeeze lemon juice over kabobs and broil on a greased rack for 3-4 minutes. Turn and brush with marinade; broil 3-4 minutes more or until shrimps are done.

NOTE: Soak bamboo skewers in water at least 30 minutes before use. They will burn if you don't.

SPICY STIR-FRIED SHRIMP

1 lb. medium shrimp in shells
2 Tbsps. peanut oil
2 Tbsps. chopped scallions with tops
1 Tbsp. Chinese salted black beans, rinsed, drained
2 tsps. minced fresh ginger
2 cloves garlic, minced
1 tsp. finely chopped fresh hot green chili pepper
1 Tbsp. sesame oil
1 Tbsp. dark soy sauce
1 tsp. Chinese chili paste
1 tsp. oyster sauce

Split shrimp through shells down center of backs to remove dark veins. Do not remove shrimp from shells or remove the legs. Wash and drain.

Heat large heavy skillet over high heat until hot enough to evaporate a bead of water on contact. Add peanut oil, swirl to coat pan evenly.

When oil is fragrant, add scallion, black beans, ginger, garlic and chili pepper; stir-fry until garlic is fragrant, about 1 minute. Add shrimp, sesame oil, soy sauce, chili paste and oyster sauce. Cook, stirring constantly until shrimp shells turn pink and shrimps feel firm when pressed between your fingers, about 4-5 minutes.

Serve shrimp in shells at room temperature or cold.

TEA-SMOKED SHRIMP

Grated rind and juice of
2 oranges
1 tsp. salt
2 Tbsps. rice wine vinegar
30 large shrimps, unpeeled

½ cup loose tea preferably, oolong or Earl Grey
½ cup sugar
1 tsp. cayenne pepper

Combine the orange rind and juice, salt and vinegar in a mixing bowl. Add the shrimps and marinate them overnight.

To smoke the shrimps, line a heavy Dutch oven with aluminum foil. Sprinkle the tea, sugar and cayenne pepper on the foil and set a rack over it. Cover the pot tightly and turn the flame to high. The sugar will melt, and the pot will start smoking. (Keep a kitchen exhaust fan going at all times to clear the smoke.) Turn off the flame, lay the shrimps on the rack, recover, and turn the flame to high. Smoke the shrimps for 5 or 6 minutes. Do not overcook, or the shrimps will become tough.

Cool the shrimps and keep refrigerated until ready to serve. They will keep in the refrigerator for about a week.

NOTE: The shrimp will turn delightfully brown and look very delicious.

TOFU AND SHRIMP WITH HOISIN SAUCE

3 Tbsps. hoisin sauce
2 Tbsps. rice vinegar
2 Tbsps. water
2 tsps. sugar
½ tsp. ground ginger
½ tsp. cornstarch
⅛ tsp. crushed red pepper
2 Tbsps. vegetable oil
14 oz. tofu, drained, cut in 1" cubes
½ lb. medium shrimp, shelled and deveined
1 clove garlic, minced or pressed
6 green onions, cut in 1" lengths

Combine hoisin sauce, vinegar, water, sugar, ginger and cornstarch and set aside. Heat 1 tablespoon oil in large skillet over medium-high heat; add tofu cubes and stir fry about 2 minutes or until lightly browned on all sides. Remove from skillet and set aside.

Add 1 tablespoon oil to skillet, stir fry garlic and shrimp for 2 minutes over medium-high heat, stirring constantly. Stir in green onion and hoisin sauce mixture and red pepper and cook, stirring until thickened and shrimp turns slightly pink, about 3 minutes. Add tofu and combine well, stirring carefully so as not to break up tofu cubes.

NOTE: If you do not like hot food, decrease the amount of crushed red pepper.

TUNA-PUFF WEDGES

1 7-oz. can tuna, drained and flaked
1½ tsps. prepared mustard
¼ tsp. Worcestershire sauce
¼ cup mayonnaise
1½ tsps. grated onion
2 Tbsps. green pepper, chopped
3 hamburger buns or English muffins, split
½ cup mayonnaise
¼ cup American cheese, shredded
6 tomato slices

Blend first 6 ingredients; pile onto bun halves. Top each half with a tomato slice. Blend ½ cup mayonnaise with the cheese and spread over tomato slices. Broil until topping puffs and browns.

When slightly cooled, cut into 4-6 wedges with a sharp knife and serve.

NOTE: You will not believe how delicious the lowly tuna can taste. Grated onion with mayonnaise does wonders for this recipe and other dips. Add enough onion so you can taste it. I found the Japanese plastic grater best for grating.

Always taste as you follow any recipe, making changes according to your taste. Mark the changes on your recipe immediately before you forget.

Mushrooms

CLAM-STUFFED MUSHROOMS

2 lbs. large mushrooms
1 8-oz. can minced clams
½ cup butter
1 clove garlic, minced
½ cup dry breadcrumbs
⅓ cup parsley, chopped
¾ tsp. salt
¼ tsp. pepper

Remove mushroom stems and place caps, rounded side down on rack of broiler pan. Drain liquid from clams and reserve. In 10" skillet, over medium heat, melt butter and brush on caps. In remaining butter cook chopped stems, garlic and clam liquid for 5 minutes. Stir in clams and remaining ingredients. Spoon into caps and broil 8 minutes until tender.

NOTE: Very good variation to stuffed mushrooms. Add grated parmesan cheese on top before broiling, if desired.

CRISPY MUSHROOM CHIPS

Nonstick cooking spray

½ lb. large mushrooms

Preheat oven to 250°. Coat large baking sheet with cooking spray and set aside. Using sharp knife, slice the mushrooms very thin, then transfer to the baking sheet, arranging the slices in a single layer. Bake, uncovered for 2-2½ hours or until crisp and completely dry.

NOTE: Check often to see it is not overdone. You will find that mushrooms, without any seasoning, have a very distinct taste which grows on you.

MARINATED MUSHROOMS

25 fresh mushrooms
1 hard-cooked egg yolk, mashed
⅓ cup wine vinegar
⅓ cup vegetable oil
½ tsp. salt
½ tsp. white pepper
2 tsps. chopped parsley
1 tsp. Dijon mustard
1 Tbsp. brown sugar

Mix together all ingredients except mushrooms. Bring to a boil and add cleaned mushrooms. Cook 5 to 6 minutes. Cool and refrigerate overnight in the marinade. Serve with toothpicks.

MUSHROOM MINI-CORNUCOPIA

Pastry Crust:

2 cups all-purpose flour
¾ tsp. salt
⅔ cup shortening
4-5 Tbsps. cold or ice water

Sift flour and salt into mixing bowl. Cut shortening in to resemble fine crumbs. Sprinkle water over the surface and mix together lightly. Gather into a ball and roll out on lightly floured pastry board to ⅛" thickness. Using a lightly-floured 1½" diameter drinking glass, cut out pastry rounds.

Filling:

2 Tbsps. butter
1 small onion, chopped fine
½ lb. fresh mushrooms, cleaned and chopped fine
Dash cayenne pepper
3 Tbsps. sour cream
1 hard boiled egg, chopped fine
1 Tbsp. cooked rice
¼ tsp. salt
⅛ tsp. black pepper
1 egg yolk, slightly beaten
1 Tbsp. cream

Melt butter in skillet. Add onions and mushrooms. Sauté 5 minutes until onions are transparent. Transfer onion mixture to mixing bowl. Add egg, rice, salt, black and cayenne pepper and sour cream. Blend thoroughly.

Place ½ teaspoon filling on center of each pastry round. Moisten two-thirds of outer edge of the rounds with water. Bring moistened edges together. Pinch, tapering the end to form a horn shape. Fold back the opposite end and leave it open. Place filled pastry horns on baking sheet. Brush with mixture of egg yolk and cream. Bake at 400° for 10-15 minutes until lightly browned.

FRENCH FRIED MUSHROOMS

⅓ cup flour
¼ cup dry bread crumbs
1½ tsps. salt
¼ tsp. white pepper
¼ tsp. thyme
¼ tsp. rosemary
½ tsp. oregano
1 lb. fresh mushrooms, cleaned, medium whole or large quartered
1 egg, lightly beaten

In mixing bowl combine flour, bread crumbs, salt, pepper, thyme, rosemary and oregano. Dip mushrooms into beaten egg. With slotted spoon remove mushrooms to flour mixture. Toss well to coat. Fry in deep hot oil until golden brown. Drain on paper towels and serve hot.

NOTE: This will replace French Fried Potatoes in your family.

ITALIAN MUSHROOMS

½ lb. fresh mushrooms or 3 4-oz. cans mushrooms, drained

¼ cup water or mushroom water

½ cup Wishbone Italian Dressing

If using fresh mushrooms, clean thoroughly with mushroom brush or crumpled paper towel and trim ¼ inch from the stem. Place in a ziplock plastic bag with ¼ cup water and bottled dressing.

If using canned mushrooms, drain, reserve liquid. Place in plastic ziplock bag with ¼ cup of the mushroom liquid and bottled dressing.

Remove all the air from the bag so marinade will completely surround the mushrooms. Refrigerate overnight and enjoy.

You may add or decrease liquid according to your taste. Shake dressing well before mixing with the mushrooms.

NOTE: I first tasted this on the mainland at the Kurata's and almost devoured a whole quart of huge, fresh marinated mushrooms. I never forgot how good they were and learned how easy they are to prepare. If you are a mushroom lover, this will become your favorite recipe.

JUANITA'S MARINATED MUSHROOMS

½ cup salad oil
⅓ cup cider vinegar
2 Tbsps. green onion, chopped
2 Tbsps. parsley, chopped
1 clove garlic, minced
½ tsp. salt
2 tsps. sugar
20 small mushrooms, sliced
1 round onion, sliced thin
2 cucumbers, seeded and sliced thin

Make marinade with oil, vinegar, green onion, parsley, garlic and seasonings. Add sliced mushrooms, onion and cucumbers and marinate 4 hours or overnight.

Serve with some of the marinade in a nice bowl.

NOTE: The cucumbers are completely different from the mushrooms both in texture and taste. You will like this and find it an instant hit.

You may add more mushrooms, onions and cucumbers to remaining marinade and have another supply of this delicious marinated mushrooms.

MUSHROOM CROWNS

24-30 medium mushrooms
1 cup lean ground pork
4 medium prawns
6-8 water chestnuts, finely chopped
1 Tbsp. dark soy sauce
1 Tbsp. Sherry
½ tsp. salt
½ tsp. sugar
1 tsp. cornstarch
2 tsps. oil
½ cup chicken stock
4-5 Tbsps. oyster sauce
1 stalk green onion, chopped

Clean and stem mushrooms. Shell and devein prawns and mince them. Mix with water chestnuts, pork, soy sauce, Sherry, sugar, salt and cornstarch. Spread about 1 teaspoonful of filling into each mushroom.

Heat 2 teaspoons of oil in skillet and place mushrooms in a single layer with the filling facing up. Brown for 1 minute. Pour ½ cup stock into skillet, cover and simmer for 8-10 minutes, adding more stock, if necessary. Uncover. (There should be about ¼ cup stock left in the skillet.) Add oyster sauce and baste the mushrooms. When sauce thickens, transfer to platter and garnish with chopped green onions.

MUSHROOM NEWBURG

¼ cup butter
1 lb. mushrooms, cleaned and halved
2 Tbsps. flour
1¼ cups milk or half-and-half
¼ cup dry Sherry
¼ tsp. salt
⅛ tsp. ground nutmeg
3 egg yolks, beaten
4 frozen patty shells, prepared according to package directions

Melt butter in saucepan. Add mushrooms and sauté for 5 minutes. Remove with slotted spoon and reserve.

Mix flour with melted butter. Slowly add milk and Sherry, stirring constantly, until smooth sauce is formed. Stir in salt and nutmeg; simmer gently for 10 minutes. Mix 3 tablespoons of this sauce into egg yolks; stir egg yolk mixture into the sauce. Add reserved mushrooms. Taste and adjust seasonings.

Cook for about 2 minutes, stirring constantly until mixture bubbles. Spoon mushroom sauce into patty shells and serve.

NOTE: In place of the patty shells use the Mini-Shrimp Tartletts pastry from PUPUS: Island Adaptations. Tartletts can be done ahead, frozen, thawed to room temperature, filled with stuffing, warmed and served.

MUSHROOMS STUFFED WITH SHRIMPS

2 Tbsps. butter, melted
12 large mushrooms, cleaned stems removed
12 medium shrimp, cooked, deveined and chopped
1 Tbsp. chives, finely chopped
1 clove garlic, finely diced
1 Tbsp. cooking Sherry
¼ cup bread crumbs
¼ tsp. salt
Parmesan cheese
Paprika

Dip mushroom caps in melted butter and set aside in greased pan.

Fry chopped mushroom stems, shrimp, chives and garlic in remaining butter until mushrooms are tender, about 3 minutes. Add Sherry and stir. Add salt and enough bread crumbs until mixture holds together.

Stuff the mushroom caps with mixture. Sprinkle tops with Parmesan cheese and paprika. Broil until hot and nicely browned.

NOTE: Mushroom lovers and shrimp lovers will really go for this dish. Not only is it delicious, but also easy to prepare.

MUSHROOMS WITH RAISINS

1 Tbsp. butter
½ lb. mushrooms, cleaned,
stems removed
3 oz. white dry wine
3 oz. catsup
2 oz. raisins

Melt butter in saucepan. Add mushrooms and gently sauté over moderate heat for 2 minutes, stirring constantly.

Add wine, catsup and raisins, simmer for 1 minute.

Pour mixture in a bowl and chill until ready to serve. Drain and serve on a bed of lettuce.

NOTE: The raisins in this recipe add a slightly sweet flavor to it and is quite nice. Tried it and liked it so here it is for you to decide.

MUSHROOMS STUFFED WITH SPINACH AND HAM

½ can cream of mushroom soup
½ tsp. salt
⅛ tsp. black pepper
Dash of nutmeg
1 pkg. 10-oz. frozen spinach
2 Tbsps. butter
2 stalks scallions, finely chopped
¼ cup cooked ham, finely diced
1 drop Tabasco sauce
¼ tsp. Worcestershire sauce
24 large fresh mushroom caps, cleaned
Bread crumbs

Cook spinach according to package directions; cool under cold running water and remove all moisture by squeezing it in the palms of your hands. Finely chop the spinach. Melt butter, add scallions and ham and sauté for 3 minutes, stirring occasionally. Add spinach and cook for 3 minutes, stirring occasionally. Stir in the mushroom soup, salt, pepper, Tabasco and Worcestershire sauces. Season mushroom caps with salt and pepper and fill them with mixture. Sprinkle bread crumbs over them, arrange on a greased baking pan, stuffed side up and bake at 350° for 15 minutes. Serve immediately.

NOTE: The original recipe called for preparing a white sauce. The cream of mushroom soup works just as well, if not better, and it certainly cuts down on the work.

NUTTY STUFFED MUSHROOMS

24 medium mushrooms
2 Tbsps. butter
1 tsp. instant minced onion
½ cup dry breadcrumbs
¼ cup sliced almonds or Brazil nuts
2 strips bacon, crisped, crumbled
¼ tsp. salt
6 Tbsps. canned chicken broth

Clean mushrooms with mushroom brush or crumpled paper towel. DO NOT WASH WITH WATER. Remove stems and chop, reserving caps.

Heat butter and sauté stems for 2 minutes. Add onions and cook another 2 minutes. Combine stems and onion mixture in bowl with breadcrumbs, nuts, bacon and salt. Add broth and mix well.

Stuff this mixture into the mushroom caps. Place in shallow, buttered dish and bake at 350° for 8-10 minutes or until heated through.

NOTE: Mushrooms are very porous and will absorb water if they are washed. This will prevent them from absorbing any seasoning you may use. They will also get slimy if washed.

Variation: You may substitute pine nuts for the almonds or Brazil nuts.

SNAILS IN MUSHROOM CAPS

1 block butter
1 Tbsp. parsley, finely chopped
2 cloves garlic, finely diced
1 scallion, white part only, finely diced
1 tsp. seasoned salt
1 Tbsp. lemon juice
⅛ tsp. black pepper
12 large canned snails, drained and cut in half
24 fresh mushroom caps, 1½" in diameter, cleaned

Blend together the butter, parsley, garlic, scallion, lemon juice and pepper. Place ¼ teaspoon of garlic butter in each mushroom cap. Place one piece of snail in each mushroom cap.

Cover the snails with the remaining garlic butter and arrange caps on small dishes or in a baking dish lined with rock salt which will hold the caps upright.

Broil 4" away from the broiling element for 4-6 minutes. The caps are ready when the butter is golden brown.

Serve hot.

NOTE: Even people with an aversion to snails will love this. Have lots of napkins handy to wipe the butter that drips from their mouths.

SPINACH-STUFFED MUSHROOMS

1 lb. medium mushrooms
1 10-oz. pkg. frozen, chopped spinach, squeezed dry
1 Tbsp. butter
2 Tbsps. flour
½ cup milk
Dash of salt
¼ tsp. nutmeg
2 egg yolks
¼ cup cooked, crumbled bacon
¼ cup Parmesan cheese, grated

Clean mushrooms with mushroom brush or brush lightly with crumpled napkin or paper towel; remove stems. DO NOT WASH.

In small pan, melt butter, blend in flour with whisk. Whisking, add milk and seasonings. Cook until thickened.

Add yolks and remove from heat. Add spinach and bacon. Cool slightly and fill caps, mounding the tops slightly.

Dust with Parmesan cheese and bake at 350° for 10-15 minutes or until cheese is melted and tops are lightly browned.

NOTE: The egg yolks and bacon add a nice flavor to this delicious stuffed mushroom recipe. Mushrooms are my favorite. I hope they are yours, too.

STUFFED BLACK MUSHROOMS

24 medium dried black mushrooms (shiitake)
½ lb. fresh shrimp
½ tsp. salt
½ white onion, minced
¼ cup fresh coriander, minced
1 tsp. ginger, finely minced
1 egg, lightly beaten
½ lb. ground pork
½ tsp. salt
1 tsp. sesame oil
½ tsp. pepper
1 Tbsp. Sherry
1 Tbsp. oyster sauce

Soak dried mushrooms in warm water about 30 minutes. Squeeze excess water; cut off stems. Shell and devein shrimps. Put shrimps in bowl with ½ teaspoon salt and gently mix with fingers. Rinse several times and drain well. Mince shrimp, onion, coriander and ginger. Beat egg slightly. Combine minced ingredients, egg and all of the remaining stuffing ingredients in a bowl and mix thoroughly. Fill the mushroom caps with stuffing, rounding off the tops. Garnish with coriander leaves. Boil water in lower section of your steamer. Line upper part with cheesecloth. Place stuffed mushroom caps in the steamer and steam, covered, for 15 minutes. Serve warm.

NOTE: Use one-third the amount of dried coriander if unable to find fresh coriander. I used ground turkey in place of the ground pork and it turned out pretty good.

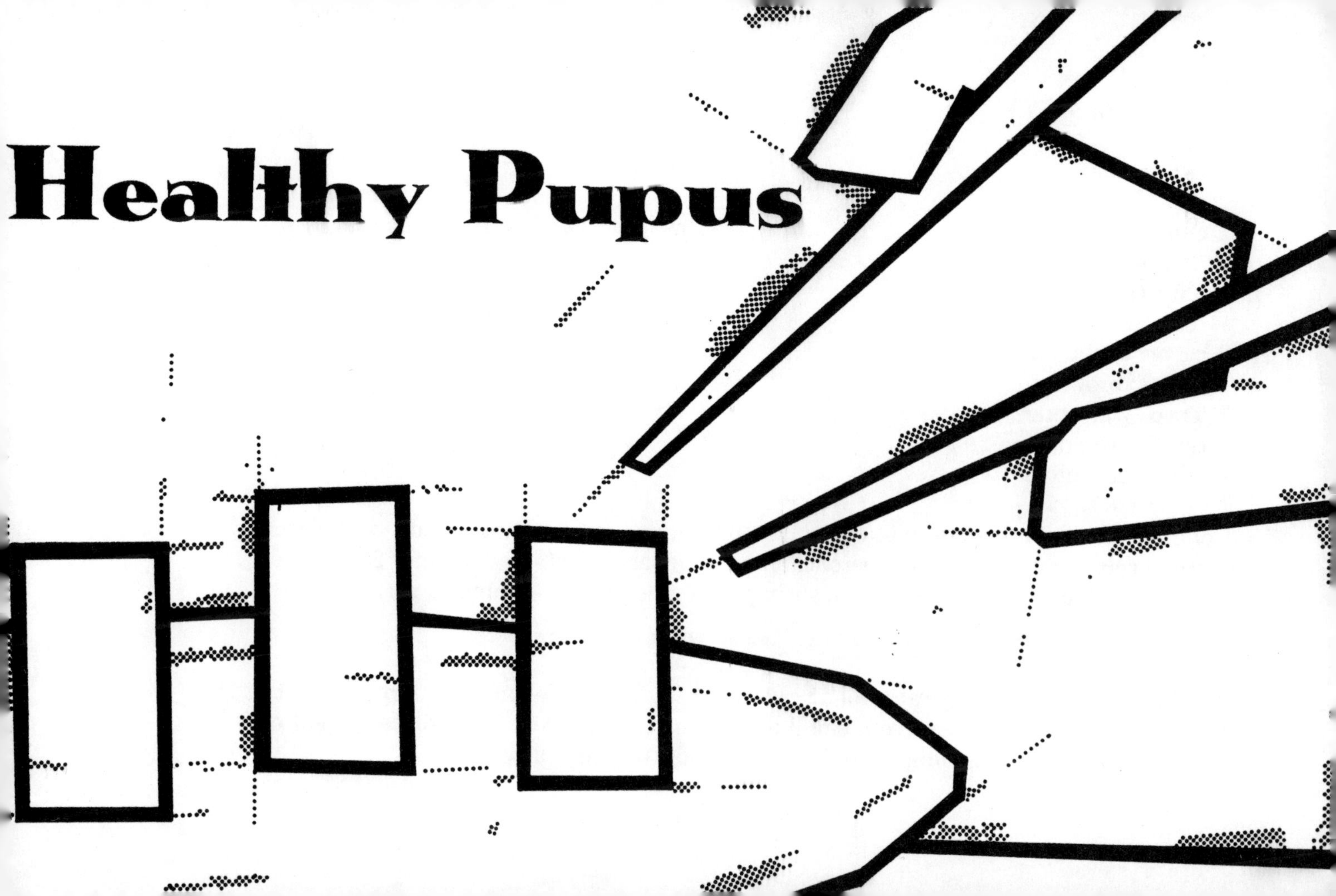
Healthy Pupus

ANTIPASTO

1 cup catsup
1 cup chili sauce
1 cup water
½ cup olive oil
½ cup tarragon vinegar
½ cup lemon juice
2 cloves garlic, minced
2 Tbsps. brown sugar
1 Tbsp. Worcestershire sauce
1 tsp. horseradish
Dash of cayenne
Salt to taste
½ head cauliflower, cut bite-size
3 medium carrots, thinly sliced
2 stalks celery, diced
½ lb. small mushrooms, trimmed
1 8-oz. jar pepperoncini, diced
1 6-oz. jar artichoke hearts, quartered
3 7½-oz. cans chunk tuna, drained
1 6½-oz. can shrimp, drained
1 lb. can cut green beans, drained

Combine first 12 ingredients in saucepan and simmer for 3 minutes. Add cauliflower, carrots, celery, mushrooms, pepperoncini and artichoke hearts and simmer 20 minutes until tender but crunchy. Add tuna, shrimp and green beans, simmer 5 more minutes.

Cool and refrigerate at least 24 hours. Serve with wheat crackers.

NOTE: Keeps in the refrigerator for at least 2 weeks. This recipe makes a large quantity so if you are planning to serve a small group, cut the recipe in half. You may add or eliminate any non-seasoning ingredient according to your taste.

DEVILED SHRIMP

12 black peppercorns
12 coriander seeds
4 whole cloves
1 bay leaf
½ tsp. each red pepper flakes, mustard seeds and crumbled dry thyme
1 medium yellow onion, chopped
1 small stalk celery, chopped
3 slices lemon
3 cloves garlic, sliced thin
⅔ cup white wine vinegar
24 large shrimp, shelled and deveined
¼ cup lemon juice
¼ cup shoyu
⅛ tsp. cayenne pepper to taste or hot red pepper sauce to taste

Place peppercorns, coriander seeds, cloves, bay leaf, red pepper flakes, mustard seeds and thyme in small piece of cheese cloth and tie securely. In a large heavy saucepan, bring 2½ cups of unsalted water to a boil over moderately high heat; add the onion, celery, lemon slices, garlic, vinegar and bag of spices.

Reduce the heat to moderate and let mixture simmer uncovered for 15 minutes. Add the shrimp and cook, uncovered, stirring often for 2-3 minutes or until they turn pink. Transfer to a large bowl and cool to room temperature. Cover and refrigerate. Drain the shrimp and place in a serving dish. Add the lemon juice, shoyu, cayenne pepper and red pepper sauce and toss to mix. Serve with toothpicks.

MARINATED MUSHROOMS

1 lb. fresh mushrooms
Juice of 1 lemon
1 lemon, cut into thin rounds
¾ cup Safflower oil
¼ cup cider vinegar
2 cloves garlic
¼ tsp. pepper
1 tsp. or less salt
Fresh parsley for garnish

Clean mushrooms; trim stems. Place in a large saucepan; toss with lemon juice. Add oil, vinegar, garlic, pepper and salt. Cook over medium-high heat 20-30 minutes, stirring frequently.

Remove from heat; cool to room temperature. Chill. Drain. Cover a serving plate with fresh parsley; top with lemon rounds. Spoon mushrooms over lemons and serve.

NOTE: These mushrooms will keep about a week in the refrigerator. Remaining marinade can be used for marinating artichoke hearts or as a salad dressing.

MARINATED SALMON

½ cup fresh lime juice
¾ cup onion, finely chopped
1 stalk celery, finely chopped
2 tomatoes, peeled and chopped
¾ tsp. or less salt
¾ tsp. pepper
1½ tsps. sugar
3-4 drops Tabasco sauce
1 lb. fresh salmon, boned, skinned and cut into 1-inch cubes
Fresh parsley for garnish
Fresh lemon wedges for garnish
Cherry tomatoes, halved, for garnish
1 white onion, sliced into rings for garnish

Combine lime juice, onion, celery, tomatoes, salt, pepper, sugar and Tabasco, pour over salmon. Toss; cover.

Chill at least 6 hours; drain.

To serve, cover a bed of fresh parsley with onion rings. Arrange salmon over top; ring with cherry tomatoes and lemon wedges.

NOTE: Serve with French bread. This is a good and healthy way to serve salmon for those who are cholesterol conscious.

STUFFED MUSHROOMS

1 lb. large fresh mushrooms
½ cup Oil and Vinegar Dressing*
1 bunch fresh spinach
½ cup Safflower mayonnaise
3 Tbsps. grated onion
1 Tbsp. lemon juice
6 oz. King Crab legs meat
½ cup grated low-fat Cheddar cheese

Clean and stem mushrooms; marinate in Oil and Vinegar Dressing for 1 hour. Drain. Wash spinach leaves; shake, but do not dry. Cook covered in heavy skillet 2-3 minutes or until wilted. Drain; squeeze out excess moisture. Chop. Combine mayonnaise, onion and lemon juice. Toss with crab and spinach. Stuff mushrooms; sprinkle with cheese. Bake at 375° for 15 minutes.

NOTE: You may omit the spinach or omit the crab and double the spinach for those who are allergic to seafood.

*OIL AND VINEGAR DRESSING

½ cup Safflower oil
¼ cup Olive oil
¼ cup cider vinegar
¾ tsp. or less salt
¼ tsp. pepper

Combine ingredients in covered jar; shake. Yield: 1 cup.

TOFU DIP/SANDWICH SPREAD

½ block tofu (approx. 10 oz.)
1 Tbsp. green onion, minced
2 tsps. garlic powder
1 Tbsp. French's mustard
2 Tbsps. mayonnaise
¼ tsp. salt
White pepper to taste

Squeeze excess water from tofu using cheesecloth or dishtowel. Mash well and mix with remaining ingredients. Use as a dip with vegetables or Oatmeal Crackers.

NOTE: When using as a sandwich spread, use 2 additional tablespoons of mayonnaise. Good with tomatoes and lettuce. Our daughter who hates tofu just loved this and sent the recipe from Honolulu.

TERIYAKI TOFU

¼ cup sesame seed
2 Tbsps. dry Sherry
2 tsps. cornstarch
⅓ cup shoyu
2 cloves garlic, pressed
¼ cup firmly packed brown sugar
¼ tsp. dry mustard
1 tsp. grated ginger
1 block fresh tofu

Cut tofu into thirds lengthwise. Drain and set aside. In small pan over medium heat, stir sesame seed until lightly toasted; remove from pan and set aside. In same pan, stir together Sherry and cornstarch; stir in shoyu, garlic, brown sugar, dry mustard and ginger and cook over medium heat until mixture boils and thickens; cool.

Fry tofu in hot oil until golden brown on both sides. Pour sauce over tofu in shallow pan and coat thoroughly on all sides; cover tightly with foil and marinate for an hour. Broil tofu on rack in shallow baking pan until sauce bubbles (about 2 minutes on each side); basting occasionally with remaining sauce. Cut into ¾-inch cubes, sprinkle with sesame seed and serve with wooden picks for spearing.

NOTE: Original recipe called for the use of aburage. I like the use of tofu better and it is an innovative way of using it.

OATMEAL CRACKERS

3 cups old fashioned oatmeal
1 cup mochiko
½ tsp. baking soda
½ tsp. salt
1 cup water
¼ cup no-cholesterol margarine

Boil water and margarine. Add to dry ingredients and mix lightly. Roll dough into quarter-sized balls and roll on baking pan to less than ¼-inch thickness. Bake at 375° for 15-20 minutes until lightly browned.

TUNA ANTIPASTO

1 6½-oz. can water-pack tuna, drained
1 15-oz. can artichoke hearts, drained and quartered
3 green onions, sliced
¼ lb. fresh mushrooms, sliced
1 8-oz. can tomato sauce
1 Tbsp. olive oil
¼ cup red wine vinegar
1 clove garlic, crushed

Combine all ingredients; chill at least 6 hours before serving.

Serve with crusty French bread for dipping.

NOTE: For variation I have used artificial crab, boiled scallops and chunky kamabuko in place of tuna which tends to get messy when you mix the ingredients.

TUNA-STUFFED CUCUMBERS

1 can 6½-oz. water-packed light tuna, drained and flaked
½ cup soft whole wheat bread crumbs (1 slice)
1 medium stalk celery, chopped fine
¼ cup finely chopped sweet red pepper
1 green onion, chopped fine
8 oz. plain low-fat yogurt
1 Tbsp. minced parsley
2 tsps. lemon juice
2 Tbsps. reduced-calorie mayonnaise
1½ tsps. peanut oil
1 tsp. Dijon or spicy brown mustard
⅛ tsp. black pepper
4 medium cucumbers

In small bowl mix all of the ingredients except the cucumbers and set aside. Halve each cucumber crosswise. Using a spoon, carefully scoop out the centers leaving shells about ¼-inch thick. Stuff the tuna mixture into each hollowed-out cucumber half.

Wrap in plastic and refrigerate at least 4 hours. Cut into ¾-inch slices to serve.

NOTE: Stuffed cucumbers will get soggy if leftover, so stuff only what you need to serve at one time.

The red pepper and green onion and parsley make it look very Christmassy. Delicious too.

ORDER BLANK

Please send me _____ copies of *Pupus . . . again* @ $9.95*

_____ copies of *Pupus: Island Adaptations* @ $9.95*

I am enclosing my check or money order for $ ________________,payable to Bess Press.

____

Name (please print)

____

Address

____

City State Zip Code

* Price includes postage and handling. Allow 4-6 weeks for delivery.

Bess Press
P. O. Box 22388
Honolulu, HI 96823

ORDER BLANK

Please send me _____ copies of *Pupus . . . again* @ $9.95*

_____ copies of *Pupus: Island Adaptations* @ $9.95*

I am enclosing my check or money order for $ ________________, payable to Bess Press.

____
Name (please print)

____
Address

____
City State Zip Code

* Price includes postage and handling. Allow 4-6 weeks for delivery.

Bess Press
P. O. Box 22388
Honolulu, HI 96823